Companion Booklet

Liturgy and Sacraments

Module Consultant
Sr. Linda Gaupin, CDP, PhD

***Echoes of Faith Plus* Program Directors**
Edmund F. Gordon, MA
National Conference for Catechetical Leadership
Jo Rotunno, MA
RCL Benziger

Content Specialist
Catherine Dooley, OP, PhD

Educational Consultant
Judith Deckers, MEd

Contributors
Rev. Louis J. Cameli, STD
Catherine Dooley, OP, PhD
Harry Dudley, DMin
Rev. Robert D. Duggan, STD
Sr. Linda Gaupin, CDP, PhD
Maureen A. Kelly, MA
Cardinal Roger M. Mahony, DD
Kate Ristow, MA
David Thomas, PhD

A Project of the
National Conference for Catechetical Leadership
Produced by RCL Benziger

Special Thanks

We wish to acknowledge the contribution of Betty Flaherty, OP, and Regis Krusniewski, SSND, who served as consultants on the original Liturgy and Sacraments module. We also wish to extend special thanks to the following individuals who appear in the bonus interviews on the DVD for this module:

Catherine Dooley, OP, PhD

Rev. Lawrence Mick, MA

Nihil Obstat
Rev. Msgr. Robert Coerver
Censor Librorum

Imprimatur
† Most Reverend Kevin J. Farrell, DD, Bishop of Dallas

February 12, 2008

The Nihil Obstat and Imprimatur are official declarations that the material reviewed is free of doctrinal or moral error. No implication is contained therein that those granting the Nihil Obstat and Imprimatur agree with the contents, opinions, or statements expressed.

Send all inquiries to:
RCL Benziger
200 East Bethany Drive
Allen, TX 75002-3804

Toll Free   877-275-4725
Fax   800-688-8356

Visit us at   www.RCLBenziger.com
              www.EchoesofFaith.com
              www.FaithFirst.com
              www.WholeCommunityCatechesis.com

Printed in the United States of America

20584   978-0-7829-1152-7

1 2 3 4 5 6 7 8 • 14 13 12 11 10 09

ACKNOWLEDGMENTS

Scripture quotations from *New Revised Standard Version Bible: Catholic Edition,* copyright 1989, 1993 Division of Christian Education of the National Council of the Churches of Christ in the United States of America. Used by permission. All rights reserved.

Excerpts from the English translation of the *General Directory for Catechesis,* copyright © 1997, United States Conference of Catholic Bishops, Libreria Editrice Vaticana. All rights reserved. No part of this work may be reproduced or transmitted in any form without the permission in writing from the copyright holder.

Excerpts from English translation of the *Catechism of the Catholic Church* for the United States of America Copyright © 1994, United States Catholic Conference, Inc.—Libreria Editrice Vaticana. English translation of the: Catechism of the Catholic Church Modifications from the Editio Typica Copyright © 1997, United States Catholic Conference, Inc.—Libreria Editrice Vaticana. All rights reserved.

Excerpts from the *Constitution on Sacred Liturgy* (Sacrosanctum Concilium) are taken from *The Documents of Vatican II,* Walter M. Abbot, S.J., general editor. New York: Herder and Herder, 1966. All rights reserved.

Excerpt from the English translation of *On Catechesis in Our Time* (Catechesi Tradendae), copyright © 1979, Libreria Editrice Vaticana. All rights reserved.

Excerpt from the English translation of *The Role of the Family in the Modern World* (Familiaris Consortio) copyright © 1981, Daughters of Saint Paul, Libreria Editrice Vaticana. All rights reserved.

Excerpts from *National Directory for Catechesis,* copyright © 2005, United States Conference of Catholic Bishops, Washington, DC. Used with permission. All rights reserved. No part of this work may be reproduced or transmitted in any form without the permission in writing from the copyright holder.

Excerpts from *National Catechetical Directory: Sharing the Light of Faith,* copyright © 1979, United States Catholic Conference, Department of Education, Washington, DC. Used with permission. All rights reserved. No part of this work may be reproduced or transmitted in any form without the permission in writing from the copyright holder.

Excerpt from *Environment and Art in Catholic Worship,* copyright © 1978, United States Catholic Conference. Used with permission. All rights reserved. No part of this work may be reproduced or transmitted in any form without the permission in writing from the copyright holder.

Excerpts are taken from the English translation of *Rite of Marriage.* International Committee on English in the Liturgy (ICEL), copyright © 1969 (ICEL); *Ordination of a Priest,* copyright ©1985 (ICEL); *Ordination of Deacons,* copyright © 1985 (ICEL); *Rite of Christian Initiation of Adults,* copyright © 1985 (ICEL). All rights reserved.

Excerpt from *A Source Book about Liturgy* by Gabe Huck. Chicago: Liturgy Training Publications, copyright © 1979. All rights reserved.

Contents

Welcome to *Echoes of Faith Plus!*

The *General Directory for Catechesis (GDC)* tells us, "The Lord Jesus invites men and women, in a special way, to follow him, teacher and formator of disciples. This personal call of Jesus Christ and its relationship to him are the true moving forces of catechetical activity" (*GDC* 231). This call needs a response from you in order to flourish. As you begin your ministry as a catechist, you will need to deepen your knowledge of the faith and of the Gospel. You will need to develop techniques and skills for presenting the faith and adapting it to your group of adults, children, or youth. Catechesis is always about communicating the faith!

Echoes of Faith Plus has been developed by the National Conference for Catechetical Leadership (NCCL) to provide you with the basic tools to begin your ministry as a catechist. It is being used in more than one hundred dioceses in the United States and Canada and has proven to be an effective process to set you on the way to have a wonderful experience as a catechist.

We have designed this program for use in varied settings. If you are working alone on a module, it is important that you link up with someone, e.g., your local DRE, catechist trainer, or parish priest. Since catechesis always involves communication, it is important that you have someone with whom to discuss your new learning, to ask questions, and to try out new ideas!

Catechesis is an activity of the whole Church. As a catechist you join a worldwide network of catechists who support each other in prayer. The Church is depending on you to bring "tidings of great joy" to the classrooms, religious education centers, homes, and wherever catechesis takes place.

May the Holy Spirit guide you, energize you, and sustain you!

Lee Nagel
Lee Nagel
NCCL Executive Director

Edmund F. Gordon
Edmund F. Gordon
NCCL Project Director

A Project of the National Conference for Catechetical Leadership Produced by RCL Benziger

How to Use
Echoes of Faith Plus

Echoes of Faith Plus is a basic-level, video-assisted resource for the formation, training, and enrichment of catechists in parish and Catholic school settings. *Echoes* was sponsored and developed by the National Conference for Catechetical Leadership (NCCL) and produced by RCL Benziger.

The *Echoes* project is divided into three series of modules. Each series relates to one of the three aspects of catechist formation explained in the *General Directory for Catechesis*—being, knowing, and *savoir-faire*. (See *GDC* 238.)

The Catechist: (being)	Three modules on the vocation and roles of the catechist, plus first steps for getting started in the ministry
Methodology: (savoir-faire)	Four modules for different grade levels of children and youth One module for facilitators of adult faith formation One overview module on human and faith development
Theology: (knowing)	Four modules treating the four pillars of the *Catechism of the Catholic Church,* plus a fifth module introducing Sacred Scripture. (Note: These modules can also be used for general adult faith formation.)

The main components of each module are:

- **A DVD.** The DVD is comprised of a four–segment video process related to the module content plus two related expert interviews.
- **A Companion Booklet.** The booklet anchors the *Echoes* process. Each booklet begins with an article for spiritual formation and a prayer. The booklet then provides a four–segment process of reflection, discussion, faith sharing, and prayer as the participant moves back and forth between the DVD and print material. Each segment includes a follow-up enrichment article. The back of the booklet offers related articles and resources. These resources and two bonus interviews on the DVD could provide material for additional sessions.
- **A CD-ROM.** The CD-ROM features compressed files that offer a way to review the basic video content of the four segments on a computer. However, it does not include the interviews found on the DVD. The CD-ROM is included at no charge with each companion booklet.

The length of time required to complete each module varies with the length of the DVD and how it is used. This module should take approximately four hours to process. The key to success with *Echoes of Faith Plus* is your willingness to engage in the complete process. Ideally, your reflection process will take place in a group setting that models the kind of Christian community you wish to establish in your own catechesis. If you must process the module alone, share your insights later in a group setting or with a friend in ministry.

> **Catechists do not merely instruct their students about Christ; they lead them to him.**
>
> *National Directory for Catechesis (NDC) 55E*

Visit http://www. EchoesofFaith.com for additional resources to enrich your catechetical ministry.

Participation in the Mystery of Christ

by Reverend Louis J. Cameli, STD

Catechists, parents, and all who want to communicate to others the Catholic faith and tradition of the liturgy and the sacraments understand instinctively that sharing information is not enough. We know that we must draw life from the liturgy and sacraments of the Church in such a way that others, too, can grasp the transforming power of the Church's sacramental life. In other words, we must be immersed in a liturgical and sacramental spirituality that shapes their lives decisively.

As noble and praiseworthy as these thoughts sound, a very practical issue remains. Where can we begin to reflect and deepen a liturgical and sacramental spirituality? How do we make explicit experiences that may be very deeply rooted within us but have not been reflected upon explicitly?

A good starting point might be St. Paul's words in his letter to the Romans: *I appeal to you, therefore, brothers and sisters, by the mercies of God, to present your bodies as a living sacrifice, holy and acceptable to God, which is your spiritual worship* (Romans 12:1). Paul's words express the "end product" of people who have engaged in the worship that is led by Jesus and prompted by the Spirit. These are people who have linked themselves sacramentally with Jesus. They have come to know the saving power of his death and Resurrection. They have understood that the death and Resurrection of Jesus are not simply events locked in a past moment in history but historical moments whose saving power is accessible to all people in all places and in every time.

The saving power of the Paschal mystery is accessible to all of us today.

In this spirit and understanding, Paul writes in the same letter of the experience of Baptism: *Do you not know that all of us who have been baptized into Christ Jesus were baptized into his death? Therefore we have been buried with him by baptism into death, so that, just as Christ was raised from the dead by the glory of the Father, so we too might walk in newness of life* (Romans 6:3–4). These words of Paul further illuminate our understanding of worship in Spirit and in truth through the sacraments of the Church. Not only does our sacramental worship help us transcend the limits of time and space and enable us to enter and participate in the mystery of Christ, this sacramental worship transforms us, changes us, *". . . so that we too might walk in newness of life."* True worship and real participation in the sacraments cannot leave us unchanged. We change and grow more deeply into conformity with the Christ whose holy mysteries we celebrate.

Notice, too, that although so much of the language is spiritual (mystery of Christ, spiritual worship), it takes place in a physical world, in tangible signs and expressions of faith, and in our very bodies. The origin of the mystery is the Incarnate Word of God, the only Son of God who took on flesh and in his body conquered sin and death. The signs and symbols of the sacraments in their physical dimensions touch our bodily existence and become vehicles that usher us into spiritual realms and transformation.

This is the heart of the spirituality of liturgy and sacraments. In physical signs and symbols we find the communication of grace that transforms us and brings us into God's very own life. Our lively sense of this reality and this spirituality will shape in ever more effective ways our communication of the liturgical and sacramental life to those entrusted to our care.

• • • **For Reflection** • • •

- Describe ways in which you have been transformed through your participation in the sacraments.
- How would you describe to a non-Catholic the importance of the Church's worship and sacramental life?

Louis J. Cameli is a priest of the Archdiocese of Chicago and pastor of Divine Savior Parish in Norridge, Illinois. He completed his theological studies at the Gregorian University in Rome and obtained a doctorate in theology with a specialization in spirituality. He is the former director of ongoing formation of priests in the Archdiocese of Chicago and director of the Cardinal Stritch Retreat House, Mundelein, Illinois. In February, 2002, he received the Pope John XXIII Award from the National Organization for the Continuing Education of Roman Catholic Clergy (NOCERCC) for his contributions to the continuing education and ongoing formation of priests. He has authored numerous books on spirituality and also served as a writer and theological consultant for RCL Benziger's *Faith First* and *Faith First Legacy Edition* K-8 curriculum.

Signs of Christ's Presence

Lord Jesus Christ,

you have **revealed** to us

the **mystery** of your Father

through your life and **saving work.**

Spirit of Christ, you **live today**

through the mysteries

of the Church's **sacramental life.**

Body of Christ,

open us to your whole Body, the People of God.

Blood of Christ, cleanse us from all sin and wrongdoing.

Your **presence** in the Eucharist

is a sign to us of your **covenant love.**

May the **Eucharist** inspire us to become signs

of your **presence** in the world as we do your will and

help your **kingdom** come throughout the earth.

Amen.

Overview: Liturgy and Sacraments

Catholics are a sacramental people. Our faith is rooted in the belief that God is present among us, that God took on flesh and walked among us in the person of Jesus Christ, that Jesus' death and Resurrection were saving for us all, and that the Spirit of God was sent by Jesus to guide and animate us as Church. When we gather to worship, we ritualize our belief in these mysteries and celebrate the ways in which we find them still deeply present in our lives. In this module you will explore the meaning of liturgy and sacrament and gain insight into why the sacramental life of the faith community is so central to our Catholic identity.

You will engage in a process of faith reflection using three components: a DVD, this companion booklet, and a CD-ROM. See page 5 for an explanation of how these components complement one another. You began the process on pages 6 and 7 with a reflection on our participation in the mystery of Christ through the sacraments. On the next two pages you will engage in an opening activity that will invite you to reflect on family rituals in preparation for your study of Catholic ritual and liturgy.

The rest of the booklet is divided into four segments that parallel the divisions of the DVD. The topics are:

1. **What Is Liturgy?**
   Part 1: Ritual and Liturgy
   Part 2: Liturgy and the Paschal Mystery
2. **Liturgy and Christian Identity**
   Part 1: Music and Sacred Space
   Part 2: Symbols in Liturgy
3. **Sacraments of Initiation**
   Part 1: The Sacramental Principle
   Part 2: Baptism, Confirmation, and Eucharist
4. **Sacraments of Healing and Service**
   Part 1: Sacraments of Healing
   Part 2: Sacraments at the Service of Communion

There is an enrichment article at the end of each segment process that extends learning by exploring a topic related to the segment theme.

This module is only a brief introduction to the Church's liturgy and sacramental life. As you continue to read, study, reflect, and attend classes and workshops, you will grow in knowledge and insight. Both adult and catechist formation requires the mutual support of other learners. Try to participate in the learning process for this module in a group setting. If circumstances require that you work independently, find at least one other person with whom you can share your reflections.

Linda Gaupin is a Sister of Divine Providence from Allison Park, Pennsylvania. She has served as chairperson of the Theology Department, La Roche College, Pittsburgh, Pennsylvania, Director of Worship, Diocese of Wilmington, Delaware, Diocesan Director of Religious Education in Orlando, Florida, and Associate Director of the Secretariat for the Liturgy, USCCB in Washington, DC. Linda is both author and lecturer on topics pertaining to liturgy and liturgical and sacramental catechesis. She holds a PhD from Catholic University of America, Washington, DC.

Before You Begin

What family rituals from your childhood do you recall? What family rituals have you observed in other families that you appreciate? List them on the chart below, then choose one of them and explain why it stands out in your memory. Write your thoughts, and then share them with at least one other person.

My Family Rituals	Rituals in Other Families

What Is Liturgy?

Human beings create rituals. We have rituals for gathering together, for celebrating key life moments, and for remembering significant events. We use rituals to pattern our lives and discover meaning within them. The patterned elements of a ritual have the power to evoke emotion, memory, and insight. Religious rituals serve the same purpose on a much deeper level. The symbols and patterned words and actions that they incorporate do more than help us feel and recall and understand. They also provide pathways into the mystery of God. They are expressions of our life and faith, and of our participation in the Paschal mystery of the dying and rising of Christ. Liturgy is the name we give to the religious rituals such as the Mass and sacraments that we celebrate as a Church community. They are our acts of public worship.

Goal

To explore the nature and use of ritual, symbols, and symbolic actions in the Church's celebration of the Paschal mystery

Learning Objectives

- To explain the nature and importance of ritual in the Church's liturgy

- To describe key elements of liturgy and their role in celebrating the Paschal mystery

- To describe how the Christian mystery is celebrated over the cycle of time

Exercise

Take a few moments to reflect on the following question. Then discuss your thoughts with another person or with your group.

Recall an experience of an Easter Vigil or Sunday Eucharist that remains in your memory. In what ways were your various senses engaged by the liturgy?

Looking Ahead

Part 1: Ritual and Liturgy

The first part of this segment explores the meaning of ritual and its place in the Church's liturgy. Below you will find an outline of the principal content of the DVD that accompanies part 1 of this segment. You may wish to refer to this outline as you watch the DVD. Below the outline, there is space for you to jot down your comments and questions that occur to you during and after the viewing.

Video Outline

- Examples of the use of rituals in everyday life and in the Church's celebrations
- Reflections by experts on the nature and importance of ritual in liturgy
- A description by a liturgical expert on the meaning of the Paschal mystery

Comments and Questions

Use the space below to list comments, questions, feelings, or ideas that occur to you as you view the video.

> **Ritual does for movement what language does for sound, transforms it from the inchoate into the expressive.**
>
> **Harvey Cox in**
> ***A Sourcebook about Liturgy***

Watch Segment 1, Part 1 of the DVD or CD-ROM now.

Looking Back

Part 1: Ritual and Liturgy

Reflect silently on one or more of the questions below and then jot down your response(s). Then share your thoughts with another person or with a group.

1. What can special family rituals teach us about the meaning of Eucharist? List at least three elements of the family ritual event in the left column below, and next to each identify in the right column what it can teach us about the Eucharistic liturgy.

Family Ritual	Eucharist

2. What image from this segment of the video stands out in your memory? What did this image communicate to you about the meaning of liturgy?

3. Read the following three statements about the meaning of liturgy. Choose one and write in your own words what it means to you.

   Liturgy is participation in work of God.
   Liturgy is a response to God's blessing.
   Liturgy makes present the Paschal mystery.

Ritual satisfies our human need for pattern, meaning, and identity.

•

Liturgical rituals provide avenues into the mystery of God.

•

The Eucharist is our central liturgical celebration.

•

We celebrate the Paschal mystery in all our liturgies.

Looking Ahead

Part 2: Liturgy and the Paschal Mystery

The second part of segment 1 explores the role of the assembly, effective proclamation of the word of God, and the celebration of the Paschal mystery in time. Below you will find an outline of the principal content of the DVD that accompanies this part. You may wish to refer to this outline as you watch the DVD. Below the outline, there is space for you to jot down your comments and questions that occur to you during and after the viewing.

Video Outline

- An exploration through word and image of the role of the assembly in the liturgy
- A discussion and demonstration of the importance of effective proclamation of the word of God in liturgy
- A description of the role of the liturgical seasons in the Church's liturgical celebration of the liturgy
- An illustration of the Liturgy of the Hours, the daily prayer of the Church

Comments and Questions

Use the space below to list comments, questions, feelings, or ideas that occur to you as you view the video.

The liturgy is the summit toward which the activity of the Church is directed; it is also the font from which all her power flows.

Constitution on the Sacred Liturgy (SC) 10

Watch Segment 1, Part 2 of the DVD or CD-ROM now.

Looking Back

Part 2: Liturgy and the Paschal Mystery

Reflect silently on one or more of the questions below and then jot down your response(s). Then share your thoughts with another person or with a group.

1. What is your responsibility as a member of the assembly for making the liturgy in your parish an effective celebration? List three specific aspects of your responsibility. Give examples of what you could do.

2. From what you learned on the video, give three reasons why the Liturgy of the Word is such an important part of the Eucharistic liturgy.

3. The wheel diagram marks the great liturgical seasons in the Church year. Mark on it one feast that was meaningful for you during the past year. In what way did its celebration deepen your understanding of the mystery of Christ?

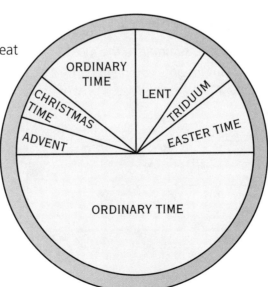

Looking Beyond

Liturgical formation . . . must explain what the Christian liturgy is, and what the sacraments are. . . . It must also however, offer an experience of the different kinds of celebration and it must make symbols, gestures, etc. known and loved.

General Directory for Catechesis (GDC) 87

FOR CATECHISTS AND PARENTS

Children enjoy participating in ritual prayer. In your home or classroom, provide ritual prayer experiences that include symbolic actions such as blessing, kneeling, or bowing.

In this segment of the module you have learned the nature of ritual, its role in the Church's liturgy, and how all the elements of liturgy work together to make present the Paschal mystery. The exercise below will give you an opportunity to reflect on the significance of some of the ritual actions used in liturgy.

CELEBRATING OUR FAITH

In the Church's liturgy such actions as gathering, listening, praising, thanking, and eating together take on great meaning. Reflect on the following human actions that also occur in liturgy. What is the significance of each of these actions when you participate in them both within and outside the Church's liturgy?

Action	Outside Liturgy	Within Liturgy
Gathering		
Listening		
Praising		
Thanking		
Eating together		

What Did I Learn?

In this space summarize the most important insights you gained in this segment.

What Will I Change?

In this space write one thing you will do differently as a catechist because of what you learned in this segment.

What Is Liturgy?

by Linda Gaupin, CDP

Liturgy is the word commonly used to describe the public worship of the Church. It is our prayer as the Body of Christ. It is the outstanding means whereby the faithful "can express in their lives, and manifest to others, the mystery of Christ and the real nature of the true Church" (*Constitution on the Sacred Liturgy* 2). Thus the *Catechism of the Catholic Church* teaches that the liturgy "makes the Church present and manifests her as the visible sign of the communion in Christ between God and men" (*CCC* 1071).

The Church has a vast treasury of liturgical prayer: the celebration of the Eucharist and the sacraments, celebrations of the Word, blessings, the Liturgy of the Hours, and the various ritual celebrations associated with the Rite of Christian Initiation of Adults. One of the principal tasks of catechesis is forming children, youth, and adults into the liturgical life of the Church.

Liturgical prayer is primarily ritual activity. It uses ritual language to speak about, proclaim, and make real the great mysteries of our faith.

Liturgy uses the language of ritual structure, symbol, gesture, word, and time to signify and proclaim the mysteries of our faith.

After Vatican Council II all of our liturgical rites were revised to include introductory rites, a Liturgy of the Word, a sacramental or liturgical action, and concluding rites. The introductory rites help us take on the form of a community, give us a common identity and purpose, and prepare us to listen to God's Word. In the Liturgy of the Word we enter into an unending dialogue between God and a covenant people where the community of faith listens to God speaking to them. Through our active participation in the sacramental action we encounter the saving mystery that is celebrated. And in the concluding rites we are sent forth to go out and live what we have just prayed, thereby assenting to the great unity between liturgy and life. Our full, conscious, and active participation throughout this basic ritual structure continuously forms and shapes us as a people.

> *Liturgy is considered the most powerful formative experience of Church.*

The primary symbols and gestures of liturgy also both form and transform us, the people of God. We are people of the *assembly* who *gather* to form the one Body of Christ. We are people of the *light* who proclaim our belief in "Christ, the light of the world" and *pass* this light on to others. We are people of the *cross* who, *marked* with this sign, live out this mystery in our daily lives.

We are people of the *water,* *immersed* forever into the Paschal mystery. We are people of the *oil,* *anointed* as Christ-figures in this world. We are people who have been *claimed by Christ and continue to be reconciled* and made one with him in the *laying on of hands.* We are people of the *white garment* who have *put on Christ.* And we are people of the *bread and wine, nourished* on the Body and Blood of Christ, who are *sent forth* to be a eucharistic people in the world. These symbols and gestures continually appear throughout our many liturgical celebrations. Our full, conscious, and active participation in these symbols and gestures never ceases to form and transform us as the people of God and followers of Christ.

Thus, liturgy is considered the most powerful formative experience of Church. Both the General Directory for Catechesis (1998) and the U.S. National Directory for Catechesis (2005) call knowledge and participation in liturgy and sacraments one of the most important tasks of catechesis. (See *GDC* 87 and *NDC* 20).

• • •   For Reflection   • • •

What have you learned from this article about the powerful role liturgy plays in the spiritual formation of a Christian?

2

Liturgy and Christian Identity

The *Catechism of the Catholic Church* tells us that "The liturgy of the Church presupposes, integrates, and sanctifies elements from creation and human culture, conferring on them the dignity of signs of grace of the new creation in Jesus Christ" (*CCC* 1149). Liturgical celebrations are a weaving together of signs and symbols drawn from our human experience, words and actions, singing and music, and sacred images. An artful blending of these elements produces a worship experience that can evoke for us the mystery of God. The way we structure our worship space helps us to connect what we live and believe with the saving activity of God in Christ. Integrating cultural elements into liturgy helps the community to understand the meaning of the Christian mystery. Indeed, the worshiping community itself is a symbol of the relationship of God and God's people.

Goal

To explore how worship expresses our identity as a faith community

Learning Objectives

- To explain the significance of liturgical space and music in liturgy

- To identify ways that cultural expression can be incorporated into liturgy

- To describe the role of the assembly in liturgical celebration

Exercise

Take a few moments to reflect on the following question. Then discuss your thoughts with another person or with your group.

In what ways has music enhanced your celebration of liturgy?

Looking Ahead

Part 1: Music and Sacred Space

The first part of this segment explores the elements of space, music and symbols in the celebration of liturgy. Below you will find an outline of the principal content of the DVD that accompanies part 1 of this segment. You may wish to refer to this outline as you watch the DVD. Below the outline, there is space for you to jot down your comments and questions that occur to you during and after the viewing.

Video Outline

- A description of the role of liturgical space as a symbol of our relationship to God in Christ
- Illustrations of the effective use of music in liturgy
- Theological and pastoral reflections on the power of good music in liturgy

Comments and Questions

Use the space below to list comments, questions, feelings, or ideas that occur to you as you view the video.

> **Because the assembly gathers in the presence of God to celebrate his saving deeds, liturgy's climate is one of awe, mystery, wonder, reverence, thanksgiving, and praise.**
>
> *Environment and Art in Catholic Worship* 34

Watch Segment 2, Part 1 of the DVD or CD-ROM now.

Looking Back

Part 1: Music and Sacred Space

Reflect silently on one or more of the questions below and then jot down your response(s). Then share your thoughts with another person or with a group.

1. What significance is there to the placement in liturgical space of each of the following elements?

Elements of Liturgical Space	Significance
Baptismal font or pool	
Seating for the assembly	
Ambo and altar	

2. If you could alter the design of the worship space in your parish, what changes would you make? How would these changes lead to more effective liturgical celebration?

3. Michael Joncas speaks on the video of four ways that music can enhance liturgical celebration. Select one or more of these functions of music from the list below and describe ways in which it has contributed to an effective celebration for you.

   Proclamation of the Gospel

   Reinforcing the Gospel message

   Fellowship/community

   Call to service

How do you tie Catholic, African traditions in the liturgies

Liturgical space helps express the relationship of the assembly to one another and to God.

•

Music is an important part of worship.

•

Music proclaims, catechizes, builds fellowship and leads to service.

Looking Ahead

Part 2: Symbols in Liturgy

The second part of segment 2 explores the use of symbols and their significance in liturgy. Below you will find an outline of the principal content of the DVD that accompanies this part. You may wish to refer to this outline as you watch the DVD. Below the outline, there is space for you to jot down your comments and questions that occur to you during and after the viewing.

Video Outline

- A description of the significance of liturgical symbols in the liturgy
- Illustration and discussion by experts of the importance of cultural expression in liturgy
- An explanation of the significance of the symbolic actions of the liturgy

Comments and Questions

Use the space below to list comments, questions, feelings, or ideas that occur to you as you view the video.

Watch Segment 2, Part 2 of the DVD or CD-ROM now.

Looking Back

Part 2: Symbols in Liturgy

Reflect silently on one or more of the questions below and then jot down your response(s). Then share your thoughts with another person or with a group.

1. Water, light, fire, and oil are universal symbols with many layers of meaning. Choose one of these symbols and write it in the center of the word map below. Around the name of the symbol, describe different meanings that this symbol can have in the Christian liturgy.

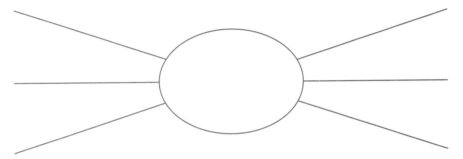

2. Recall a cultural symbol used in the Native American liturgy in the video. Describe ways in which that symbol might enhance the worship experience for the Native American community.

3. The assembly and the actions it performs at liturgy express the relationship between God and God's people. In what ways can an understanding of this principle by the people enhance the celebration of liturgy?

Looking Beyond

In this segment you learned about the importance of environment, music, and the use of symbols in the celebration of liturgy. The exercise below will give you an opportunity to reflect on your responsibility for the effective celebration of liturgy.

> **It is the whole community, the Body of Christ united with its head, that celebrates.**
> CCC 1140

CELEBRATING OUR FAITH

Reflect on your role as a member of the assembly at Sunday liturgy. What practical steps can you take to participate more actively and thereby make liturgy more meaningful for the entire community?

FOR CATECHISTS AND PARENTS

The space for communal prayer in your classroom or home is important to the celebration. Take care in creating this sacred space and choose elements that will enhance the experience.

What Did I Learn?

In this space summarize the most important insights you gained in this segment.

What Will I Change?

In this space write one thing you will do differently as a catechist because of what you learned in this segment.

The Role of the Assembly

by Cardinal Roger M. Mahony

The Second Vatican Council called for the "full, conscious, and active participation by all the faithful" at the liturgy (*Constitution on the Sacred Liturgy* 14). Here are several habits that each churchgoing Catholic can begin to cultivate that will bring us together into a life-giving liturgical practice Sunday after Sunday.

Become people who worship in the midst of the Sunday liturgy. Prepare by using the Sunday Gospel and New Testament letter in your daily reading. Bring to the prayer of intercession on Sunday all that you pray for; take from it persons to be remembered daily by you. Hear the daily news of your community and the world as a Christian called to lift up the world's needs in prayer. Mark with prayer your morning rising and your evening going to bed: the Lord's Prayer certainly, but also some song or psalm from the Sunday liturgy.

Become people who prepare for Sunday Liturgy and for whom Sunday Liturgy is preparation for the week. Seek little ways that can help make the Lord's Day a day when liturgy has room. Find some habit for Sunday morning that helps you anticipate joining the community at liturgy and stretch toward the Reign of God we glimpse at Mass. It might be a way to make more real the Sunday collection for the Church and the poor, or of extending the peace of Christ you receive each Sunday to others in need of that peace. It might be fasting from food or distractions to become thoroughly hungry for God's Word and the Eucharistic banquet. It might be to form the habit of blessing your children, a practice that is so much to be praised in Hispanic families.

At the liturgy, be the Church. Know the awesome responsibility you share for making this liturgy! Do not hide; do your private praying in the other hours of the week. Welcome one another, be at peace with one another. Sit together. Sing songs from your heart. Do not be afraid to show, in your eager attention, that you are hungry for God's Word when the readers read; hungry for Christ's Body and Blood when you come forward in procession to receive Holy Communion. Give thanks and praise

Cardinal Roger M. Mahony a native of Los Angeles, was named the Cardinal Archbishop of Los Angeles in 1991. He was ordained a priest in the diocese of Fresno, California in 1962, and appointed Auxiliary to the Bishop of Fresno in 1975. He served as Bishop of Stockton, California from 1980 to 1985, when he was appointed Archbishop of Los Angeles.

Cardinal Mahony's many committee memberships for the National Conference of Catholic Bishops have included the areas of liturgy, pro-life activities, sexual abuse, migration and refugees, HIV/AIDS, and communications. He has served as a member of the Catholic Common Ground Initiative and of the advisory board for the Bernardin Center for Theology and Ministry. Cardinal Mahony has a long history of leadership in issues related to the social teachings of the Church.

to God by your great attention in the Eucharistic Prayer. Keep your eyes open to one another and do everything you can to build up the Church, the Body of Christ. If the presider or homilist needs help, do not criticize—help.

Know the awesome responsibility you share for making this liturgy!

Apart from the liturgy, be the Church. Remember we are always the Body of Christ in communion with one another. In the simplest deeds of daily life, at work or at home, be conscious of this life we share in Christ. Look at the liturgy as a remote preparation for your week. Listening to God's Word on Sunday is preparation for listening for God's Word in our lives all week. The thanks we proclaim at the Eucharistic Prayer is a preparation for thanks we offer every day. The common table of Holy Communion is a preparation for looking at the whole world.

Give thanks always. Pray grace at meals, even when you are alone. Sing when you are with others at table. Permeate your morning prayer and night prayer with praise and thanks to God. Enrich it with verses of psalms and prayers from the tradition. Cultivate moments of contemplation even during the busiest day, when gratitude can flow from the goodness of a person, any element of creation, or any good work of human making.

• • • *For Reflection* • • •

What good habit will you try to form to make your participation at Sunday Eucharist more complete?

Sacraments of Initiation

3

The principle of sacramentality is at the heart of our understanding of how God is present to us in the created world. All that exists gives evidence of the reality of God. In the Church's understanding, the signs and symbols of a sacrament have the power to make present the reality which they signify. The person of Jesus Christ fully reveals to us the mystery of God. We can say, then, that Jesus is the sacrament of God. The Church, in the same sense, is the sacrament of Jesus Christ, since she continues Christ's presence in the world. The Church in turn has identified seven sacraments through which God is revealed to us in order to strengthen us, nourish us, and call us to fullness in the life of Christ. In the sacraments we celebrate and give thanks for God's saving presence in Jesus Christ through the Spirit.

Goal

To explore the relationship among the three Sacraments of Initiation and to appreciate the centrality of Eucharist in the Christian life

Learning Objectives

- To express a basic understanding of the concept of sacrament

- To describe the role of the three Sacraments of Initiation in the process of conversion

- To articulate the relationship between the Liturgy of the Word and the Liturgy of the Eucharist

Exercise

Take a few moments to reflect on the following exercise. Then discuss your thoughts with another person or with your group.

Describe a place or moment in your life other than the Eucharist when you have experienced the presence of God.

Prayer

Ever-present God, you speak to us through all the wonders of your creation. We thank you for all your gifts, but especially for the gift of your Risen Son, whose presence we celebrate through the sacraments. Through the gift of your Spirit, help us reflect your image to others in all we do and say. We ask this in Jesus' name. Amen.

Looking Ahead

Part 1: The Sacramental Principle

The first part of this segment begins with a prologue that describes the principle of sacramentality and the Church's teaching about the nature of the sacraments. Below you will find an outline of the principal content of the DVD that accompanies part 1 of this segment. You may wish to refer to this outline as you watch the DVD. Below the outline, there is space for you to jot down your comments and questions that occur to you during and after the viewing.

Video Outline

- A reflection in words and images describing God's presence in all of creation.
- A description of the sacramental principle
- A definition of sacrament and the role of signs and symbols in the seven sacraments

Comments and Questions

Use the space below to list comments, questions, feelings, or ideas that occur to you as you view the video.

Watch Segment 3, Part 1 of the DVD or CD-ROM now.

Looking Back

Part 1: The Sacramental Principle

Reflect silently on one or more of the questions below and then jot down your response(s). Then share your thoughts with another person or with a group.

1. The video states that the Church can be seen as the sacrament of Jesus in the world and that Jesus is the sacrament of God. In light of this, in what ways can you say that you are a sacrament of Christ in the world?

2. The pouring of water, the lighting of fire, and anointing with oil are symbolic actions used in the celebration of the Sacraments of Initiation. Choose one of these actions and explain what it signifies in the process of conversion.

Elements	Significance
Pouring of water	
Lighting of fire	
Anointing with oil	

3. In the video, Father Tom Caroluzza points out that catechumens are formed as Catholics in four key ways. Under each item in the list below, tell how has each of these activities contributed to your own formation as a Christian.

   Living with the Community

   Learning with the Community

   Praying with the Community

   Serving the Community

Remember . . .

All that exists holds evidence of the mystery of God.

•

The sacraments use signs and symbolic actions to make present Christ's saving action.

•

The Church is the sacrament of Jesus.

•

Jesus is the sacrament of God.

Looking Ahead

Part 2: Baptism, Confirmation, and Eucharist

The second part of this segment explores the relationship among the three Sacraments of Initiation: Baptism, Confirmation, and Eucharist. Below you will find an outline of the principal content of the DVD that accompanies this part. You may wish to refer to this outline as you watch the DVD. Below the outline, there is space for you to jot down your comments and questions that occur to you during and after the viewing.

Video Outline

- An explanation of the three Sacraments of Initiation and the role of the RCIA process in the process of conversion
- A description of the Eucharist as the source and summit of the Christian life
- Illustrations and presentation on these two parts of the Mass
- A reflection on the ways in which we are called to live the Eucharist

Comments and Questions

Use the space below to list comments, questions, feelings, or ideas that occur to you as you view the video.

> The sacraments of Christian initiation—Baptism, Confirmation, and the Eucharist—lay the *foundations* of every Christian life.
> **CCC 1212**

Watch Segment 3, Part 2 of the DVD or CD-ROM now.

Looking Back

Part 2: Baptism, Confirmation, and Eucharist

Reflect silently on one or more of the questions below and then jot down your response(s). Then share your thoughts with another person or with a group.

1. What is the significance of each of the three Sacraments of Initiation in the initiation of a Christian?

   Baptism

   Confirmation

   Eucharist

2. Complete in your own words each of the following statements describing the Eucharistic prayer.

   We praise and thank God for . . .

   We ask the Holy Spirit to . . .

   We remember that . . .

   We pray for . . .

3. Whoever receives the Body of Christ becomes the Body of Christ. How can you see this demonstrated in your life and in the life of your parish community?

Looking Beyond

In this segment you have learned more about the three Sacraments of Initiation and why the Church teaches that the Eucharist is the source and summit of the Christian life. The exercise below will help you to apply what you have learned to your own life of faith.

CELEBRATING OUR FAITH

For you, what would be three personal implications of taking seriously the Third Commandment to honor the Lord's Day? Which of these are you willing to act on right away?

FOR CATECHISTS AND PARENTS

Challenge young people by posing the question with them in the Celebrating Our Faith activity. Encourage them to follow through on their ideas.

What Did I Learn?

In this space summarize the most important insights you gained in this segment.

What Will I Change?

In this space write one thing you will do differently as a catechist because of what you learned in this segment.

Sacraments of Initiation

by Maureen A. Kelly

In Roman Catholic theology, Baptism, Confirmation and Eucharist are called the Sacraments of Initiation. Why? Precisely because the definition of initiation is "to make a member." It is these three sacraments that make individuals full members of the Church. To fully understand what this means we need to go back into the early history of the Church.

In the first three hundred years of the early Church people who wanted to belong to the Church were invited into a process of initiation called the catechumenate. It was a lengthy process during which those to be initiated were called to conversion and formed in a specific way of life by the community. The early Christian communities set up ways of being in relationship with these inquirers that showed them firsthand what living a Christian life entailed. They came to know the Lord Jesus through living the community's life of prayer and apostolic witness. They heard the stories of what Jesus had accomplished in his life, and how the Risen Christ continued to be present in the Church.

The early Christians nurtured the conversion of inquirers. They celebrated that conversion and full membership in a celebration at Easter time. The ritual celebrations of initiation, or membership, at that time included anointing with oil both before and after Baptism with water; laying on of hands; the sign of peace; and the culmination of initiation by sharing in the Lord's Supper, the Eucharist. In those early days the sacraments we know as Baptism, Confirmation, and Eucharist were celebrated in one event. They were presided over by deacons and bishops.

As the Church grew, small Christian communities grew larger. Christianity became a recognized religion. Gradually this process of initiation changed. The element of conversion to a specific way of life and the discipline of the catechumenate was lost. Receiving people into the Church became more common during the liturgical year. The ritual action of celebrating the Sacraments of Initiation at Easter became divided into separate rites, especially in the

Maureen Kelly has been involved in the ministry of Christian initiation and religious education since 1974 at local, diocesan, national, and international levels. Maureen has served as associate director of the North American Forum on the Catechumenate, as catechetical advisor and as Director of Product Management for two major catechetical publishing companies, and as Diocesan Director of Religious Education for the Diocese of Grand Island, Nebraska. She is the author of several books on the children's catechumenate. She holds a master's degree in theology from the Catholic University of Louvain, Belgium.

western Church where the bishop became the ordinary minister of Confirmation. In those communities Baptism was separated from Confirmation.

As infant baptism became more the norm, the Western Church also began to elongate the initiation process for children by raising the age for participation in the Eucharist. For the most part, the Eastern Church kept the rites of initiation intact. In the Eastern Church infants were baptized, confirmed, and received the Eucharist in the same celebration.

On December 4, 1963, during the Second Vatican Council, the *Constitution on the Sacred Liturgy* was promulgated. It mandated the restoration of the catechumenate and the revision of all of our sacramental rites. In 1972, as a result of that mandate, the Church issued the Rite of Christian Initiation of Adults (RCIA), which restored the catechumenate for unbaptized adults and children of catechetical age.

The RCIA restored initiation as a norm for the catechesis and celebration of the sacraments of Baptism, Confirmation, and Eucharist, whether they are celebrated with the unbaptized or with people baptized as infants. The change in the rite of Baptism for infants and Confirmation for those baptized as infants shows the return to the theology of initiation.

The changes in the rites and the return to a theology of initiation is something we are still working through as a practice. It was a radical departure from the way we had been preparing people for and celebrating Baptism, Confirmation and Eucharist. Much has been done to integrate this theology into our practice, and much work still remains.

● ● ● ◆ *For Reflection* ◆ ● ● ●

What experience have you had with the Rite of Christian Initiation of Adults? How would you compare it to your own experience of entry into the Christian community?

4

Sacraments of Healing and Service

The Sacraments of Initiation are the sacraments through which we enter into new life in Christ and join the community of Christian believers. All the other sacraments relate to these two and celebrate the ongoing process of conversion that Christians experience throughout their lives. The Sacrament of Penance and Reconciliation and the Sacrament of the Anointing of the Sick respond to the resulting need for strength and healing. Through them Jesus' ministry of healing and salvation continues.

The Sacrament of Penance and Reconciliation celebrates God's forgiveness with the community. Through this sacrament sinners are reconciled in their relationship with God and the community. The Anointing of the Sick is directed toward the strengthening of those experiencing physical or spiritual illness. The Sacraments of Holy Orders and Matrimony are called Sacraments at the Service of Communion. These two sacraments, which celebrate the Christian vocations of priesthood and marriage, consecrate members of the Church for service to the whole Church. Baptism is the foundational sacrament for all Christians.

Goal
To relate the Sacraments of Healing and the Sacraments at the Service of Communion to Jesus' ministry

Learning Objectives
- To explain the significance of the two Sacraments of Healing to the ongoing life of the Church
- To describe the principal responsibilities of the Catholic priesthood
- To articulate the significance of the vocation of Christian marriage for the Church

Exercise
Take a few moments to reflect on the following. Then discuss your thoughts with another person or with your group.

Recall a moment of reconciliation that you have had with another person. What did this act of reconciliation make possible for you and for the other person?

Prayer

Healing Lord, in your wisdom you have given sacraments of healing and service to assist us in our ongoing conversion into your Way. Through your Spirit, strengthen us for the work of healing division within ourselves, in our families, and in our community. Strengthen especially those among us whom you have chosen to serve as priests, deacons, and married couples. We ask this in the name of your Son. Amen.

Looking Ahead

Part 1: Sacraments of Healing

The first part of this segment explores the Sacraments of Healing and their significance in the life of the Church. Below you will find an outline of the principal content of the DVD that accompanies part 1 of this segment. You may wish to refer to this outline as you watch the DVD. Below the outline, there is space for you to jot down your comments and questions that occur to you during and after the viewing.

Video Outline

- A theologian discusses the role of grace in the process of ongoing conversion.
- A reflection on the relationship of the Sacrament of Penance and Reconciliation to the work of justice
- Two pastors reflect on their work in administering the Sacrament of Penance and Reconciliation.
- An explanation of a broader understanding of the role of the Anointing of the Sick in the Church's ministry of healing
- A description and illustration of the role of the assembly in the celebration of the Anointing of the Sick

Comments and Questions

Use the space below to list comments, questions, feelings, or ideas that occur to you as you view the video.

> **The beginning of good works is the confession of evil works. You do the truth and come to the light.**
>
> **St. Augustine**
> *In evangelium Johannis tractatus*
> **12, 13, 35, 1491**

Watch Segment 4, Part 1 of the DVD or CD-ROM now.

Looking Back

Part 1: Sacraments of Healing

Reflect silently on one or more of the questions below and then jot down your response(s). Then share your thoughts with another person or with a group.

1. What reasons can you give for why the *Catechism of the Catholic Church* now calls the first Sacrament of Healing "The Sacrament of Penance *and* Reconciliation"?

2. What are the ways you ask for, receive and offer reconciliation and forgiveness in your daily life?

3. In the space below, create a symbol for each of the two Sacraments of Healing that could help others understand the effects of these two sacraments.

   Penance and Reconciliation   **Anointing of the Sick**

Remember . . .

The Sacraments of Healing are "Penance and Reconciliation" and "The Anointing of the Sick."

•

The Sacraments of Healing reveal to us the support of the Christian community.

•

Penance and Reconciliation continue Jesus' healing mission.

•

The Anointing of the Sick is directed toward healing of both body and spirit.

Looking Ahead

Part 2: Sacraments at the Service of Communion

The second part of this segment explores the Sacraments at the Service of Communion. Below you will find an outline of the principal content of the DVD that accompanies this part. You may wish to refer to this outline as you watch the DVD. Below the outline, there is space for you to jot down your comments and questions that occur to you during and after the viewing.

Video Outline

- An explanation of the Sacraments at the Service of Communion as means of calling certain people into communities of ministry to serve the ongoing life of the Church
- An explanation and illustration of the role of the priest as presider and animator of the community
- An exploration of the biblical foundations for our understanding of Christian marriage
- A presentation and illustration of the Church's teaching on the Christian home as the domestic Church

Comments and Questions

Use the space below to list comments, questions, feelings, or ideas that occur to you as you view the video.

Holy Orders and Matrimony . . . confer a particular mission in the Church and serve to build up the People of God.

CCC 1534

Watch Segment 4, Part 2 of the DVD or CD-ROM now.

Looking Back

Part 2: Sacraments at the Service of Communion

Reflect silently on one or more of the questions below and then jot down your response(s). Then share your thoughts with another person or with a group.

1. A key role of the priest is to animate and call forth the gifts of the parish community. What gifts have been called forth from members of your parish for service to the people of God?

2. The Church teaches that a Christian home is to be a center of faith, an illustration of the Christian life, and a welcoming presence for others. How have you seen these values reflected in your own family and in those of your friends?

3. In the circle diagram mark some key moments in your sacramental life as a Christian. Choose one of these moments and in the space below describe why you chose it for your chart.

Remember . . .

The Sacraments at the Service of Communion are Holy Orders and Matrimony.

•

The hierarchal priesthood serves the common priesthood of all the laity.

•

The covenant of marriage is based on human dignity, love, commitment, and mutual fidelity.

•

The Christian witness of a married couple continues Jesus' ministry of service.

- Greeting and blessing by the priest
- Reading from Word of God
- Invitation to repentance by the priest
- Confession of sins and acceptance of penance
- Absolution by priest
- Dismissal and blessing by priest

FOR CATECHISTS AND PARENTS

Children learn what they live. Offer them opportunities to participate with the community in the Sacraments of Healing. Point out examples of service by priests and married people.

Looking Beyond

In this segment you learned more about the Sacraments of Healing as continuations of Jesus' ministry of healing and salvation. The exercise below will allow you to apply what you have learned to a concrete situation.

CELEBRATING OUR FAITH

A friend tells you that she has not celebrated the Sacrament of Penance and Reconciliation in years because she prefers to ask God's forgiveness in the privacy of her heart. What could you say to persuade her of the positive value of this sacrament?

What Did I Learn?

In this space summarize the most important insights you gained in this segment.

What Will I Change?

In this space write one thing you will do differently as a catechist because of what you learned in this segment.

Signed with the Cross of Christ

This service of signing of the forehead and senses with the sign of the cross is adapted from one of the rites of the Christian Initiation of Adults. Celebrate it with others in your faith community to recommit yourself to the faith of the Church into which you were welcomed at your Baptism.

Leader: Father of love and mercy, we thank you
for your guiding presence in our lives.
We praise and bless you, Lord.

All: We praise and bless you, Lord.

(Leader invites those assembled to face each other in pairs, and to sign each other with a cross in turn as the leader prays the following series of petitions.)

Leader: Receive the cross on your forehead:
by this sign of his love
Christ will be your strength.
Learn how to know and follow him.

Receive the sign of the cross on your ears:
may you hear the voice of the Lord.

Receive the sign of the cross on your eyes:
may you see with the light of God.

Receive the sign of the cross on your lips:
may you respond to the Word of God.

Receive the sign of the cross on your chest:
may Christ dwell in your heart by faith.

Receive the sign of the cross on your shoulders:
may you accept the sweet yoke of Christ.

Let us pray.

All: Father, may we who have been signed with
the cross of our Lord Jesus Christ,
be faithful to your teachings by its power.
May we live always by its saving power
and reveal it in our lives. Amen.

Based on "Signing of the Candidates with the Cross," *Rite of Christian Initiation of Adults*

The Sacraments at the Service of Communion

by Harry Dudley

I remember a Charles M. Schulz cartoon where the character said, "I love mankind; it's people I can't stand." Holy Orders and Matrimony (Marriage) celebrate that in the Christian life one can not separate the love of humankind (universal love) from the love of people—each person (particular love). The very name given Holy Orders and Matrimony in the *Catechism of the Catholic Church* (CCC), the Sacraments at the Service of Communion, indicates that the graces of these sacraments set aside some members of the Church to work for the good of the whole Church, the communion of all believers in Christ.

The Sacraments of Christian Initiation (Baptism, Confirmation, and Eucharist) join a person to Christ and to the body of Christ, the Church. The Sacraments of Healing (Penance and Anointing of the Sick) reconcile a baptized person with the Church when their relationship has been broken or weakened by sin. Celebrating Anointing of the Sick also strengthens their faith in Christ during illness. In Holy Orders and

Marriage, the Church prays that the Holy Spirit strengthens the baptized to serve the spiritual good of the Church.

Holy Orders

Holy Orders is the sacrament of the Church in which a baptized man is ordained and consecrated to serve the Church as a bishop, priest, or deacon. Bishops share in the fullness of Christ's priesthood and continue the work of the Apostles. They work in communion with the Pope, the successor of Saint Peter the Apostle. They authentically teach the faith, proclaim and preach God's word, lead us in celebrating the sacraments, and guide us in living the Gospel.

Priests are co-workers with their bishop. They preach God's word and lead us in the celebration of the sacraments. In the rite of the ordination of a priest, the ordaining bishop prays: "Renew within him the Spirit of holiness. / As a co-worker with the order of bishops / may he be faithful to the ministry that he receives from you, Lord God, / and be to others a model of right conduct. / May he be

Harry J. Dudley, D.Min. is currently the Director of Religious Education for the Archdiocese of Washington. He has been married for 30 years. He has worked in the catechetical ministry for over forty-two years and in diocesan ministry for the past nineteen years. His service has extended to the Archdiocese of Baltimore, the Diocese of Lafayette-in-Indiana, and the Archdiocese of Indianapolis before moving to his present position in Washington, DC.

faithful in working with the order of bishops, / so that the words of the Gospel may reach the ends of the earth, / and the family of nations, / made one in Christ, / may become God's one, holy people (*Ordination of a Priest* 22).

Deacons help bishops and priests. They proclaim God's word and can baptize and marry people. At the ordination of a deacon the Book of the Gospels is presented to them with the command, "Receive the Gospel of Christ, whose herald you now are. / Believe what you read, / teach what you believe, / and practice what you teach." (*Ordination of Deacons* 21)

Matrimony

In the Sacrament of Matrimony a baptized man and a baptized woman commit themselves to a life-long relationship. They receive the graces to always love each other, to be open to beget children within that loving relationship, and to become signs of Christ's love for the Church. The married Christian couple forms a new family in the Church and become a "church of the home," or domestic church. During the marriage rite one of the blessings prayed over the couple is: "May the peace of Christ dwell always in your hearts and in your home. / May you have true friends to stand by you, both in joy and in sorrow. / May you be ready and willing to help and comfort all who come to you in need. / And may the blessings promised to the compassionate be yours in abundance." (*Rite of Marriage* 37)

To Build Up the People of God

In each of the Sacraments at the Service of Communion, one's life is no longer one's own. Holy Orders and Matrimony confer a particular mission in the Church. Christian married couples give themselves to the service of each other and the Church. Bishops, priests and deacons are consecrated to dedicate their lives for the benefit of the whole Church. Both the love that leads to Holy Orders and the love that leads to Matrimony are authentic and expressions of God's faithful and life-giving love for all people. For God's love is both universal and particular. All authentic love is caught up into divine love. (See *Gaudium et Spes* 48.)

Holy Orders and Matrimony confer a particular mission in the church.

For Reflection

- How have married couples you know witnessed to the particular love of Christ for his Church?
- When has a priest helped you call forth your gifts to proclaim the Gospel as a catechist or in other ways?

The Paschal Mystery: God's Blessing

by Catherine Dooley, OP

Catherine Dooley, OP, is a Sinsinawa (Wisconsin) Dominican Sister. For many years Sister Catherine served as associate professor of catechetics and liturgy in the Department of Religion and Religious Education at the Catholic University of America, Washington, DC. Sister Catherine has published widely in catechetical and liturgical journals and written a number of texts and resource materials for liturgy, catechesis, and religious education. Sister Catherine holds a master's degree and a PhD from the Catholic University of Louvain, Belgium, and master's degrees from Harvard Divinity School and the Catholic University of America.

Paschal mystery is one of those realities that we teach and experience but often cannot describe. The *Catechism of the Catholic Church* places the Paschal mystery in the context of the biblical understanding of blessing. Think of the last time that you said, "That was such a blessing for me!" When you remember that event or person that was a blessing for you, you will have some idea of why the Catechism offers blessing as a description of Paschal mystery. A biblical understanding of blessing, which includes praise, thanksgiving, and acknowledgment of dependence upon God, presumes that we have experienced and recognized God's life-giving action in our lives. Blessing, then, is something we have known and acknowledged.

The ongoing story of salvation shows us that "[f]rom the beginning until the end of time the whole of God's work is a *blessing*" (CCC 1079). It is God who blesses all created things, who blessed Abraham, the patriarchs, and the people of Israel, all that they experienced from birth to aging to death. God creates in love;

God sustains in love. God's people have received blessings; therefore they are to bless. The people of Israel bless their children; leaders and kings bless their people. Immersed in the blessings from God, the people send the blessings back to the source.

Blessing, therefore, has two aspects. When applied to God, it means God's initiative, God's saving action in our lives now. On our part, it designates our own response and surrender to God our Creator in thanksgiving for God's saving presence with us.

In the liturgy of the Church, God's blessing is fully made known and communicated. We praise our God, our Father and Creator, as the source of all blessings. We give thanks for God's merciful and saving actions in our lives.

In the Eucharistic liturgy we celebrate and make present what God has done in Christ, God's blessing, the Paschal mystery. The Paschal mystery is unique; it is a historical event that occurred in the past but cannot remain in the past. By dying Christ destroyed death; by rising he restored life. Jesus, the Son of God who became incarnate, died, and was raised out of love for us, fills us with many blessings. "Through his Word, he pours into our hearts the Gift that contains all gifts, the Holy Spirit" (CCC 1082).

In the Eucharistic liturgy we recall all that God has done for us in Christ through the Spirit. We celebrate the mystery of Christ's death and resurrection, a mystery which is the paradigm for the true ultimate meaning of Christian life. Our celebration sends us forth to enter the mystery of Christ's dying and rising in our daily lives.

The Paschal mystery is the lens through which we view and interpret our human experience. Living the Paschal mystery is a "letting go."

It means coping with the inevitable fact of our own mortality and that of those whom we love. The Paschal mystery means that in the midst of pain and disappointment, there is the possibility of change and new life. The rising of the Paschal mystery means reconciliation, fidelity, forgiveness, and hope in the face of adversity. We die to our enslavements in order to live in the freedom with which Christ has made us free. The Church proclaims and celebrates this Paschal mystery in the liturgy in order to live from it and carry on God's blessings in the world.

> *The Paschal mystery is the lens through which we view and interpret our human experience.*

For Reflection

What insight have you gained into how we live the Paschal mystery in our daily lives?

The Domestic Church

by David M. Thomas

David M. Thomas has served as a graduate professor of church leadership and family life at Regis University in Denver, Colorado. He is a well-known expert on family life and the Church who has offered workshops throughout the United States, Canada, and Europe. He is the author of ten books and over two hundred articles. David served as a theological advisor for the United States Bishops' Delegation to the Vatican Synod on the Family in Rome in 1980. David and his wife Karen are the parents of six children and have opened their home to over seventy-five foster children.

According to the Book of Genesis, Adam is not only the father of all humankind, he is also the one who names all the animals. Naming was and remains an important part of life. The naming of something creates part of its identity. NASA uses words like *challenger* or *voyager* when it names its spacecraft. It does not call them *worm* or *turtle.*

In the documents of Vatican II a special name was given to the Christian family. It was called the *domestic church.* This was not a totally new name, but one that was resurrected from the treasury of ideas and language found in the early Fathers of the Church. This treasure hunt for lost, but still important ideas about the nature of the Church was typical of the work of Vatican II. We as Church were invited to go back and explore our roots and foundations so as to bring the Church into closest proximity with its head, Jesus Christ.

The early Church was quite different from what we see today. It was small and considered a minority phenomenon. It was very intentional about its life. Part of its distinctive difference was the way it organized itself as a community. In its earliest manifestations, it was much more a community of equals than it would later be. It was deeply conscious of the words of Jesus, "For where two or three are gathered in my name, I am there among them" (Matthew 18:20).

As the Church reflected on the times when gathered people became Church, it saw the life of the Christian family as one of those times. So without hesitation, it simply called the family a church, the church of the home. The adjective *domestic* meant familial.

Wanting the fullest possible awareness of our identity as Church, the bishops of Vatican II consciously chose to name the family a Christian community in its own right in chapter 11 of *The Dogmatic Constitution on the Church* (Lumen Gentium). The same language has been used by all succeeding popes into our own day. Pope Paul VI spoke about the domestic church in his teaching on evangelization, *Evangelii Nuntiandi,* where he states that "the various aspects of the entire church are present in the domestic church" (71).

Papal teaching refers to the Church as a worshiping community, an evangelizing and catechizing community, and a ministerial community. All these aspects of the Christian life happen within the family. It happens in the life of the parish and diocese as well, of course, but it often happens most within the family.

John Paul II mentioned the family as the domestic church probably a thousand times. Two themes recur in his teaching: the dignity of the human person, and the essential role of the family in preserving the connection between love and life. His major work on the family was written after the World Synod on Family Life which took place in the Vatican in 1980. After that meeting he wrote an apostolic exhortation on the family, *Familiaris Consortio (The Community of the Family)*. In it he said, "[T]he Christian family is grafted into the mystery of the Church in such a degree as to become a sharer, in its own way, in the saving mission proper to the Church" (49).

Naming the family the domestic church is an intentional use of language, describing the holiness of the place where most of Christian life happens.

Naming the family the *domestic church* is an intentional use of language, describing the holiness of the place where most of Christian life happens. Remember, Jesus himself spent most of his life in exactly such a community.

For Reflection

What can your family do to communicate to others that you are a domestic church?

The Sacraments of Healing

by Rev. Robert D. Duggan

Rev. Robert D. Duggan is a presbyter of the Archdiocese of Washington, D.C. Fr. Duggan has a License in Sacred Theology from the Gregorian University in Rome and a Doctorate from the Catholic University of America. Fr. Duggan has written and spoken extensively for many years on topics related to sacraments and liturgical renewal.

In its treatment of the seven sacraments, the *Catechism of the Catholic Church* (nn. 1420–1532) groups the sacraments of Penance and Anointing of the Sick together under the heading "The Sacraments of Healing." The close connection of these two sacraments is rooted in the ministry of Jesus, whom the Gospels describe as reaching out to heal all who were wounded by either sickness or sin.

Although in Jesus' time people generally saw illness as the effect of sin in a person's life, the Lord himself rejected this view (see John 9:2–3) and treated illness as a physical evil rather than a moral fault. Nonetheless, the Gospels describe how Jesus' ministry was directed toward all who were wounded, either by sickness or by sinful behavior. That ministry of compassion was precisely what the Lord passed on to his disciples, commanding them to perform the same works of healing that he himself engaged in (Mark 6:7–13). Jesus' gift of the Spirit after his resurrection entrusted to the apostles and their followers his own divine power for healing and reconciliation (Acts 3:1–10; John 20:19–23).

In the process of continuing and ritualizing Jesus' ministry of compassionate healing over many centuries, the Church has celebrated what we now call the sacraments of Penance and Anointing. Bishops and priests are the ordinary ministers of the Sacrament of Penance. Those who are truly sorry for their sins, who confess with a firm purpose of turning away from sin, and are willing to do the penance given them by the minister of the sacrament receive sacramental absolution of their sins. That sacramental forgiveness pronounced in the name of Christ and his Church brings the sinner both pardon from God's mercy and reconciliation with the Church. The liturgical renewal of Vatican II has given us three forms in which this sacrament may be celebrated: (1) Reconciliation of Individual Penitents [offered weekly in most parishes]; (2) Reconciliation of Several Penitents with Individual Confession & Absolution [offered in

Advent & Lent in most parishes]; and (3) Reconciliation of Penitents with General Confession & Absolution [offered only rarely under extraordinary circumstances].

The ritual for anointing (formerly called Extreme Unction) was also renewed after Vatican II and directed more towards the healing of illness than prayer for the dying. The ordinary ministers of the Sacrament of Anointing of the Sick (bishops or priests) are directed to encourage the faithful to be anointed at the onset of serious illness, rather than waiting for the point of death. The reason for this is that the purpose of the Sacrament of Anointing is healing, while Eucharist as viaticum is the specific sacrament for the dying, meant to prepare the faithful Christian to "pass over" to the Father in heaven. Anointing is a sacrament of healing because it offers to one who is ill a real grace of strengthening, both on the physical and on the spiritual levels. By a particular gift of the Holy Spirit, the Lord means to heal the person who has been made vulnerable to discouragement and temptation through suffering. If such is God's will, a healing of body often occurs by the grace of this sacrament, and if the person has committed any sins they too will be forgiven (James 5:15). The sacrament helps those who are sick to join their sufferings with the Passion of Jesus and—should their illness be terminal—helps to prepare them to depart this life.

Jesus' ministry of compassion was precisely what the Lord passed on to his disciples, commanding them to perform the same works of healing that he himself engaged in (Mark 6:7–13).

• • • **For Reflection** • • •

How has your understanding of the sacraments of healing been expanded by this article?

Seven Sacred Signs:
Teaching Sacraments Across the Grades

by Kate Ristow

Kate Ristow is National Catechetical Consultant for RCL, a contributing editor and feature writer for *Catechist* magazine, and a frequent speaker at national and regional conferences. Kate has written catechetical resources for every elementary grade level and has worked in religious education for more than thirty years as a classroom teacher, a catechist, and an administrator. Kate has a BA from Marquette University and a master's degree in religious studies from Mundelein College. She is married, is the mother of three adult sons, and has five grandchildren.

Several years ago, my husband and I attended a First Eucharist celebration. The children were a sight to see, looking solemn, innocent, and excited all at the same time. My favorite part of the liturgy was the pastor's dialogue homily with the children. He asked questions about the Eucharist and what they had done to prepare to receive the Body and Blood of Christ. Through his prompting and the children's eager responses, the pastor inventively reminded the entire assembly why the Eucharist is central to our lives.

The experience reminded me that learning about the sacraments is a life-long endeavor. To ensure that students really grow in their understanding of these saving rites, catechists need to focus on sacramental catechesis at every grade level, every year. Below are ideas for teaching the sacraments. Choose those that work best for you, but don't be timid about trying new strategies of your own.

Catechetical Content

One of the challenges catechists face in teaching the sacraments is that kids may say, "We already know this." While it is true that students may have learned something about Baptism or Reconciliation, for example, in an earlier grade, they have not learned everything. What we teach second graders about Reconciliation is not adequate for fifth graders; what we teach fifth graders about this same sacrament is not sufficient for eighth graders. The sacraments need to be taught using a spiral approach which guarantees that content is fully developed over the entire catechetical program. This gives students the opportunity to build on previous learning and to develop a fuller understanding of the significance of the sacraments in Catholic life.

Guest Speakers

Guest speakers can help you to bring parish celebrations of the sacraments to life. Invite a Minister of Care to speak about visiting the sick and how the parish celebrates the communal Anointing of the Sick. Members of the Marriage Ministry can outline how engaged couples prepare for Matrimony. A member of the Baptismal Ministry can talk about the joy of working with parents who are preparing for the Baptism of their infants. The possibilities are almost limitless! Ask speakers to bring to class objects they use in their ministry. For example, a

Minister of Care might bring a pyx to show the students; a priest can show the students a stole and explain why he wears it when celebrating Reconciliation with parishioners.

Sacramental Saints—Sharing biographies of the saints with students helps them recognize how these models of faith lived sacramental lives. Blessed Mother Theresa is a prime example of care for the sick and dying. Saint John Vianney dedicated much of his priestly ministry to absolving and counseling sinners who visited him from all over France. Saint Katherine Drexel gave her fortune to educate and house poor Native Americans and African Americans. Her life reminds us that, through Baptism, God calls each of us to live our faith by caring for others. Provide biographies of the saints to groups of older students. Invite them to find saints who lived sacramental lives. Ask each group to find at least one saint and explain how he or she exemplifies the spirit of a sacrament.

Art Activities—Following a unit on the sacraments, have students use white shelf paper to create a seven-panel mural that depicts the reception of a sacrament or a symbol for each sacrament. Students can also make posters that illustrate the different parts of sacramental rites. The completed posters can be used as colorful teaching tools for younger students learning about a sacrament for the first time.

Ritual Celebrations

The *General Directory for Catechesis* acknowledges that sacramental, or liturgical catechesis requires us to teach others about the sacraments. However, the Directory also reminds us that our catechesis must "offer an experience of the different kinds of celebration and it must make symbols, gestures, etc. known and loved" (*GDC* 87).

Bring good experiences of ritual celebration to your catechetical setting. Incorporate the ritual actions that young people will experience at Mass— walking in procession, bowing, signing with the cross, genuflecting, kneeling, blessing, and sitting in silence. These actions need not add a great deal of time to your prayer service and they will make their participation in the Sunday celebration more meaningful.

All of these strategies are designed to help children appreciate the great Paschal mystery that we celebrate in all the Church's liturgical celebrations.

For Reflection

- What is your most effective strategy for teaching the sacraments to your students?
- What ideas do you have for incorporating good experiences of ritual prayer in your classroom setting?

Resource Bibliography

Church Documents

Abbot, Walter M., SJ, gen. ed. *The Documents of Vatican II.* New York: Herder and Herder, 1966.

Benedict XVI. *Deus Caritas Est (God Is Love).* Vatican City: Libreria Editrice Vaticana, 2006.

———. *Spe Salvi (On Christian Hope.)* Vatican City: Libreria Editrice Vaticana. Washington, DC: USCCB, 2008.

Bishops' Committee on the Liturgy. *Built of Living Stones: Art, Architecture, and Worship.* Washington, DC: United States Conference of Catholic Bishops, 2001.

———. *Catholic Household Blessings and Prayers.* Washington, DC: United States Conference of Catholic Bishops, 2007.

Catechism of the Catholic Church, Second Edition. Libreria Editrice Vaticana. Washington, DC: United States Catholic Conference, 2000.

Compendium: Catechism of the Catholic Church. Washington, DC: United States Conference of Catholic Bishops, 2005.

Compendium of the Social Doctrine of the Church. Vatican City: Libreria Editrice Vaticana, 2004.

Congregation for the Clergy. *General Directory for Catechesis.* Vatican City: Libreria Editrice Vaticana, 1997.

Connell, Martin, ed. *The Catechetical Documents: A Parish Resource.* Chicago: Liturgy Training Publications, 1996.

International Commission on English in the Liturgy. *Book of Blessings: Study Edition.* Collegeville, MN: The Liturgical Press, 1989.

National Directory for Catechesis. Washington, DC: United States Conference of Catholic Bishops, 2005.

United States Catholic Catechism for Adults. Washington, DC: United States Conference of Catholic Bishops, 2006.

Theological Resources

Barnes, Michael. *In the Presence of Mystery: An Introduction to the Story of Human Religiousness.* Mystic, Conn.: Twenty-third Publications, 1984.

Ciferni, Andrew D. "Word, Liturgy of the." *The New Dictionary of Sacramental Worship,* Peter E. Fink, ed. Collegeville: The Liturgical Press, 1990.

Dallen, Rev. James. *Gathering for Eucharist: A Theology of Sunday Assembly.* Ormand Beach: Pastoral Arts Associates, 1997.

Duffy, Regis, OFM. *The Liturgy in the Catechism.* New York: Geoffrey Chapman, 1995.

Hixon, Barbara. *RCIA Ministry: An Adventure Into Mayhem and Mystery.* San Jose: Resource Publications, 1989.

Huck, Gabe, ed. *Environment and Art in Catholic Worship.* Chicago: Liturgy Training Publications, 1994.

Huck, Gabe, ed. *A Sourcebook about Liturgy.* Chicago: Liturgy Training Publications, 1994.

Huebsch, Bill. *Vatican II in Plain English.* Three volumes. Allen, Tex.: Thomas More, 1997.

Johnson, Lawrence J. *The Word and Eucharist Handbook.* San Jose: Resource Publications, 1995.

McBride, Alfred, O.P. *Essentials of the Faith: A Guide to the Catechism of the Catholic Church.* Huntington, Ind.: Our Sunday Visitor, Inc., 1994.

Osborne, Kenan B., OFM. *Christian Sacraments in a Postmodern World: A Theology for the Third Millennium.* New York: Paulist Press, 1999.

———. *Sacramental Guidelines: A Companion to the New Catechism for Religious Educators.* New York: Paulist Press, 1995.

Marini, Archbishop Piero. *A Challenging Reform: Realizing the Vision of the Liturgical Renewal, 1963–1975.* Collegeville: The Liturgical Press, 2007.

Videos

The Mystery of Faith: An Introduction to Catholicism. A ten-part video series featuring Father Michael Himes. Fisher Productions, Box 727, Jefferson Valley, New York 10535.

The Faithful Revolution: Vatican II. Allen, Texas: RCL Enterprises, Vatican II Productions, 1997.

Computer Resources

Catechism of the Catholic Church for Personal Computers. United States Catholic Conference, 1994. Available on disk and CD/ROM in English, Spanish, French.

Destination Vatican II. CD/ROM. Allen, Tex.: RCL • Resources for Christian Living, 1997.

Certificate of Completion

_____

Name

has successfully completed the process
for the Liturgy and Sacraments module
in the Echoes of Faith Plus program.

This certificate of completion is given at

_____

Parish

_____

Diocese

_____

Signature

_____

Date

Feedback Form

We hope that you have benefited from your use of this *Liturgy and Sacraments* module. Please take time to fill in your comments to the questions below. They will help the *Echoes of Faith Plus* team in planning additional resources to assist you in your ministry. If possible, discuss your responses with your program director before you mail it.

Thank you,
The *Echoes of Faith Plus* Team

1. Briefly describe your prior knowledge regarding the Church's liturgy and sacraments.

   _____

   _____

   _____

2. Name three things that you learned in this module that will be most helpful to your growth in faith.

   _____

   _____

   _____

3. What would be a good next step for your continuing growth in knowledge of liturgy and sacraments?

   _____

   _____

   _____

4. If you are a catechist, in what ways will the knowledge you gained in this module be helpful to you in your ministry?

   _____

   _____

   _____

Tear out this sheet, fold and tape it closed, and return it to us. There is a business reply mechanism on the back of this page. Or you may fill out this survey online at www.EchoesofFaith.com. Thank you.

NO POSTAGE
NECESSARY
IF MAILED
IN THE
UNITED STATES

BUSINESS REPLY MAIL

FIRST-CLASS MAIL   PERMIT NO 100   ALLEN TX

POSTAGE WILL BE PAID BY ADDRESSEE

ATTN PUBLISHER

ECHOES OF FAITH® PLUS PROJECT

RCL BENZIGER

PO BOX 7000

ALLEN TX 75013-9972

-- *Fold* --